No Suprises

Leading in the Non-Profit World

By Gloria L. Kelley
with Thomas H. Berliner, PhD

DEDICATION

I am fortunate to love my work. That has only been possible because of my loving family. I especially want to thank my husband, Dean Kelley, for encouraging me and for providing wonderful feedback on the manuscript. Lexi, my daughter, has done exceptional work that has helped bring this book and my Website together. I am a proud mom. I also want to thank Tom Berliner who believed from day one when I walked into his MBA classroom that I should do more to share my experiences and to help others learn from what has and has not worked leading an organization. Tom's constant coaching and gentle nudges were needed in helping me balancing life and work. I will forever be grateful to have learned from the best.

In addition to the three of them, I dedicate this book to every existing and wannabe leader who is committed to serving others, both your end users and your team. If that's where you are headed, then you've got the right destination.

ACKNOWLEDGEMENTS

There are SO MANY people who have helped me grow that I could write a book in just listing them. However, I do want to especially thank a few.

- The CASA Kane County Board of Directors who have served generously and tirelessly over the years.

- My CASA Kane County Team, both past and, especially, present.

- The CASA Kane County Chairman's Advisory Panel.

- Tim Barry – He has helped me take positive steps in my leadership development.

- To my girlfriends – Who without their laughter, tears and support I know I would not have had the courage to push myself to be in the beautiful place I am today.

To everyone else who offered ideas, provided feedback, tested possibilities and helped move the process along...Thank you.

CONTENTS

PROLOGUE

Leadership is intended to be visionary – to embrace the past, work with the present and plan for the future. The CASA movement was begun in 1977 by Seattle Judge David Soukup. He had a vision for every child that came into abuse and neglect court to have someone looking out for their needs. CASA Kane County came into existence in 1988. I took the position as Executive Director of CASA Kane County in March of 2007. At the time, the organization was well respected with the majority of the part-time, high performing staff members being loyal, well-educated and possessing great attitudes.

However, there was still much to be done for the organization to achieve its ultimate potential as a high-performing organization. In 2007, there were 10 part time staff members, 12 board members, 200 volunteers serving 450 children on a limited budget with a minimal amount of reserves for a rainy day. Today, there are 21 full-time staff members, 25 board members, 225 volunteers serving 550 children on a budget that has increased 600% with an endowment for long-term sustainability to serve the mission as long as the need is there.

This growth and stability are certainly not the doing of one person. Instead, it has been a one-step-at-a-time tactical progression with an eye on ever-ambitious strategic targets. What I share with you in this book has helped move CASA Kane County from where it was to where it now is. Further, it has allowed us to be confident that the future promises to be even brighter than it is today. And that's good news for the children.

I encourage you to achieve similar or even greater success. Hopefully, this book will help you do so.

"The world cares very little about what a man knows; it is what a man is able to do that counts."

Booker T. Washington

"You can't live a perfect day without doing something for someone who will never be able to repay you."

John Wooden

"There never was a person who did anything worth doing, who did not receive more than he gave."

Harriet Ward Beecher

"Nobody made a greater mistake than he who did nothing because he could do only a little."

Edmund Burke

"If your actions inspire others to dream more, learn more, do more and become more, you are a leader."

John Quincy Adams

"Vision is number one. Whatever decision that we make has to be in the best interests of the children and the organization that we protect."

Gloria L. Kelley

I

INTRODUCTION

1. Welcome

What a delight to have you read this book. I have been pushed for a long time to share my knowledge and experiences with others throughout the non-profit world. Truthfully, I didn't feel as though what I had to offer warranted such public sharing. Then a number of people whom I greatly respect pointed out areas that could benefit an interested audience.

Once I sat down and started to outline what I might share, it reinforced the encouragement that I had been hearing. Yes, I do have things to share with my counterparts at both large and small non-profit organizations. My objective is to offer these things so that you can assess their value in your environment. In the end, perhaps you will toss some of this, use some of it and, overall, feel that reading this was time well spent.

As for those of you in the *for*-profit world, I also believe that there are things for you to take away from this reading. To a certain extent, leading is leading. [You will see considerably more on this in the next chapter.]

Each chapter in this book has a specific purpose. Before turning to them, let me touch on a few important points in order to better set the table for what you will read in the individual chapters.

2. Not an Academic Undertaking

People have been studying leadership for a really long time. In doing so, many approaches to what leadership is, how it can be classified, how it can be identified, how it can (or cannot) be developed, how it relates to its environment and many other methodologies have been advanced. Virtually all institutions of higher education, both inside and outside the business world, have courses and even complete programs aimed at leadership. Truly, the information and methodologies can be overwhelming.

My MBA is in Leadership. I have studied it with a commitment greater than every other academic field to which I have been exposed. To me, it is fascinating...and ever evolving. However, this book is not about leadership history or theories (with one exception that follows shortly). It is about practical application because, to my way of thinking, if leadership cannot be applied, then what's the point?

My expectation is that you will read this book and find things valuable to your environment. When you do, I hope that you will want to share them with me at my Website *(www.glorialkelley.com)*. In doing so, your experiences can be told and others can benefit from them. There are few things that cement a suggestion better than good examples of how it succeeded.

3. The Great Man

The history of leadership is a fascinating one, spanning from the origin of man right up to this very moment. Those who study it have come up with many stages and approaches. The basic challenge involves the question: Are leaders born (i.e., with traits) or made (i.e., developed)? If born, then it is necessary to find these people to lead. If made, then it is necessary to train people to lead. Most people agree that it is a combination of the two. But let me throw in an additional thought.

Whichever of these three (born, made or a combination) you advocate, that is by no means the end of the discussion. The prevailing thought is that, once you find a leader, he/she will do the right things. The fact of the matter is that leaders make immense mistakes and there are dozens, if not hundreds, of examples. Winston Churchill is esteemed because of his unwavering leadership of Britain through the Second World War. However, if you look at his track record, he had more failures than successes in his performance. So why is he so highly venerated? [I am not singling out Prime Minister Churchill. There are many others who have the same negative balance when measuring achievement versus disappointment.] Let me provide an explanation.

Although I promised that this book would not be about theories, I want to introduce one that is essential: The Great Man Theory says that a 'leader' is the one who sees the path and directs his/her followers to victory, be it in a literal or figurative way. That's not the case, as the above contention puts forth. Instead, it is the hope and confidence that a leader gives his/her followers that inspires *them* to achieve the success that the leader wants. In other words, the leader can be wrong and still succeed.

Superior leadership definitely requires encouragement. But it isn't so much about the outward display of leadership, such as big pep talks and over-the-top pats on the back. Instead, exceptional leadership is making certain that all the stakeholders - especially your team, donors and volunteers - find personal meaning in what they do.

Since the leader need not be the single visionary, correct in every assessment, why then does The Great Man Theory still prevail? That is somewhat still a mystery. Perhaps it is because people are slow to change. Look how long it is taking for servant leadership to be adopted in spite of head-to-head comparisons that demonstrate the surpassing performance of it.

What's the point that I am trying to make? It's this: Success is more about your inspiring your team than performing your routine leadership duties. But, just like the born-made debate, it is but one ingredient in the complicated recipe. Leaders can recover from incorrect decisions but not from dashing the optimism and sureness of their followers. Make certain that what you do for your team heavily includes hope and confidence.

4. Pedal to the Metal

A few reminders. First, successful leadership is not a nine-to-five job. Anyone who thinks otherwise is in for a very rude awakening. Second, effective communication (both the how and when) is absolutely critical to the long-term success of the organization. Third, avoid at all costs the arrival of self-satisfaction. Complacency is simply not in my vocabulary and shouldn't be in yours either.

I see my job as instilling drive and urgency into accomplishing what I know needs to happen. Instead of being ego driven, become goal driven, thus accomplishing the bigger picture and more meaningful goals. Bottom line: Walk the walk and do whatever is needed to have your team accomplish the things that are important for your organization.

I am so happy when my team scores a huge win, especially when they are called upon to invest extra time and effort. When this happens and team members receive well-earned recognition, everyone wins, especially those to whom your organization has its greatest responsibility, in our case abused and neglected children.

5. Climbing Mount Everest

Mount Everest, located in the Himalayas, is Earth's highest mountain above sea level. It was first conquered by Sir Edmund Hillary in 1953. Since then, climbing to its peak has been the dream for all serious mountaineers. All of us have aspirations. I call these our Mount Everests. For some people, it might mean amassing large sums of money, maybe in the multi-millions. For others, large sums might be $10,000. Everything is relative. The point is that we all have desired destinations. Getting to them is a step-by-step affair. If you don't take steps, you won't make progress. It's as simple as that. Or, in keeping with this metaphor: "No climbing, no peaking." This goes for whatever one wants to do.

I wasn't born with a silver spoon in my mouth; far from it. [I share a little bit about that on the Website.] However, early on, I developed a strong work ethic, one that believed and still believes that the way to cross either the figurative or literal finish line requires focus, intelligence, common sense and perseverance. In other words, if you want to be the best leader you can be, then it will be small, sure steps that will get you there. Your reading books like this one and constantly striving to make yourself one smidgen better each day is the way to achieve that.

Perseverance is a real key. Synonyms, each hopefully encouraging you, include determination, doggedness, drive, endurance, grit, persistence, resolve and tenacity. You have to work at it each and every day. You have to be pleased but not content with your progress.

I once heard a cute story that has stuck with me: There are three types of people...
  a. Those who make things happen;
  b. Those who watch things happen; and
  c. Those who say 'What happened?'
Commit yourself to being in the first category.

6. Non-profit, Not-for-profit and For-profit Organizations

People often ask me: "What are the leadership differences between non-profit, not-for-profit and for-profit organizations?" Let me give you my standard answer: "It shouldn't be different." If you treat everyone who works with you as though they are a volunteer, you will be remarkably ahead of bosses who believe that positional power is the credential.

That being said, let's begin with the legal differences between the three. *Non-profits* are usually 501(c) 3 organizations and are set up to do charitable work. Although each may have paid employees, most of the staff is made up of volunteers. There are no shareholders. They rely on donations and grants, the former being tax deductible. CASA (Court Appointed Special Advocates) is the non-profit that I lead.

Not-for-profit organizations have members who receive income after expenses. There are no donations. It is a business, not a charity. Most credit unions and community hospitals are good examples of not-for-profit organizations.

For-profit organizations have as their primary motivation the maximization of profit. [In recent years, some organizations have elevated the objective of social responsibility. Nevertheless, profits are their raison d'être, their foremost purpose.]

Think of it this way: Non-profits cannot exist without donations, not-for-profits without members and for-profits without earnings. As for the leadership of each, I don't make material distinctions and suggest you not do so either.

7. Mission and Vision

In *Alice in Wonderland*, there is a scene where Alice cannot decide which path to take. The Cheshire Cat appears in the tree and asks her where she wants to go. She is unable to tell him. His reply is classic: "If you don't know where you are going, any road will take you there." It's the same for any organization. Without a destination (mission), sustainable success is very unlikely.

There is no universally accepted definition of either mission or vision. Depending on which academic book you read or corporate executive you ask, the two words are often used interchangeably. Thus, let me give you two words of caution:

1. Create a definition for each and make certain that everyone in your organization understands which is which in your world.

2. When you are speaking with someone outside your organization, clarify which is which in their minds so that the conversation can be one of the apples to apples variety.

This book adheres to the majority definitions. A *mission* explains a formal summary of the aims and values of a company, organization and even individual. It usually remains unchanged over time. It is intended to be inspiring and motivating. It usually is provided in one sentence, giving the reader the big picture of what your organization is all about. A *vision* explains a company's road map. It identifies stakeholders, processes and metrics. A vision will likely change over the course of time. A mission is who you are and a vision is what you would like to achieve or accomplish. Beneath these come things like goals, objectives, strategies, tactics, etc.

There are some great mission statements such as: American Heart Association: *To build healthier lives, free of cardiovascular diseases and stroke;* Mayo Clinic: *To inspire hope and contribute to health and well-being by providing the best care to every patient through integrated clinical practice, education and research;* and Special Olympics: *To transform communities by inspiring people throughout the world to open their minds, accept and include people with intellectual disabilities and thereby anyone who is perceived as different.*

Taglines also serve a very important purpose that complements the mission and vision. Here are a few examples of great ones: TED: *Spreading Ideas;* Alzheimer's Association: *A world without Alzheimer's*; and Human Rights Campaign: *Equality for everyone*. Within the past year, our National Organization adopted a new one "Change a Child's Story." It's so meaningful and is used in all of our publications, marketing ads and much more.

When CASA Kane County was first clarifying its mission, there was much discussion and comparison to other CASA organizations to see what had already been created. Along with those listed above, we studied what organizations were using, both inside and outside of the profit world. Again this year, we sat down with our leadership, volunteers and staff to revisit both the mission and vision because where we were 15 years ago is drastically different compared to where we are today. It was an exercise well worth conducting. If you lead an organization that hasn't done a reevaluation in a number of years, considering doing one.

During our research, we arrived at the credo that Johnson & Johnson created. It inspired us to develop our philosophy statement, one that prominently hangs in our office hallway. You can go to J&J's Website to see its philosophy statement. Boiling it down to a digestible size, here it is: *Our credo/philosophy challenges us to put the needs and well-being of the people we serve first.* Isn't that terrific?

It is essential (I would use a stronger word if I could think of one) that you have a mission statement, whether you call it a mission or a vision. Many an organization faded into oblivion because they had no clear idea as to where they were headed. Tactical changes only make sense if the long-term objective is clear. What it also provides is focus, especially when you find yourself in the weeds. As a leader in a dynamic environment, you cannot predict what will come at you at any given time. Before reacting emotionally, stop, go back to the mission statement and use it as the framework for your response.

Mission and vision are the driving forces that give the organization its purpose and direction. Program delivery and impact give non-profits their primary reasons for existence. Strategic relationships, finance and internal operations are all necessary mechanisms to achieve the organization's ends. Absent any of these, the organization will flounder and will not reach its full potential. Leadership and governance are the lubricants that keep all the parts aligned and moving.

There is one additional, very important point that I want to emphasize. Although the mission is the sine qua non of the organization, this does not mean that those served are the only ones whose needs have to be met. It is the leader's obligation to address the needs of *all* the stakeholders, including the community, the donors, the volunteers and the employees. As a side note, too often, I see where volunteers and employees are not given their due (especially recognition) and are simply treated as a means to an end. Nothing could be more short-sighted than doing this.

8. Titles and Roles

CASA Kane County is a non-profit organization that prevents children from falling through the cracks of the heavily populated court and child systems. This is done by providing each child with the voice of a well-trained volunteer advocate. Meeting the needs of children is our priority.

Removal from a family of origin is always a traumatic event that can create lifelong problems for a child. In some cases, a family can be provided resources, support and services that will help a troubled family system find healthy ways to interact and provide care. There are many possible positive outcomes for a child. Adoption, reunification, independent living or guardianship with relatives are the most viable answers to the child's need for a safe, permanent home.

In our case, the direct beneficiaries are the over 500 children annually who are protected from further abuse and neglect by the Juvenile and Probate Court system.

The court benefits from our work as we assist judges in making difficult decisions, including the determination of the child's immediate living situation, planned permanent placement and services needed. The entire community benefits in the long run as children who are given a better life will grow into happier, healthier and more productive adults who provide positive care and support for their children, rather than continuing the cycle of abuse.

My title with CASA Kane County is Executive Director. Although this title is quite common, its significance is shared with others, such as CEO, President, Principal and so on. Some non-profits simply do not assign titles to anyone, their executives included. [For a number of reasons, I kind of like this approach in select circumstances.] The point to be made is that the specific title is not critical. If everyone in the organization knows where the buck stops, feels as though they have the ear of the leadership team and are focused on the vision, then whatever you call me, we will succeed.

But I will add one side note. Sometimes, titles are important to external stakeholders, especially contributors to your financial objectives. Factor this in when you create and assign titles to your organization's workers, full-time, part-time and volunteers.

Okay, with that as an introduction, I invite you to value and enjoy what follows. Some will be old news to you. Some will be a good refresher. And some will be *Holy Cow!* material. I hope that most of it falls into this third category. Once again, my Website is *www.glorialkelley.com*. I encourage you to contact me. Aside from appreciating your feedback, I hope that you will contribute to this body of knowledge. I know that you have thoughts that are important to share.

KEY POINTS

1. Leaders must create hope and confidence in their team members. This is more important than the individual decisions that they make.

2. Leaders can recover from incorrect decisions but not from dashing the optimism and sureness of their followers.

3. There are both similarities and differences between non-profit, not-for-profit and for-profit organizations. The leadership likenesses far outweigh the distinctions.

4. Make certain that everyone in your organization not only understands the differences between mission and vision but can effectively explain them to others.

5. Regardless of how you define your hierarchy, make certain that everyone has the same definition for each term. Mission-vision-goals-objectives-strategies-tactics is a common hierarchy.

6. Titles can be beneficial or not. Give thought to which titles are appropriate for which positions.

"Start by doing what's necessary; then do what's possible; and suddenly you are doing the impossible."
Francis of Assisi

"As we look ahead into the next century, leaders will be those who empower others."
Bill Gates

"By failing to prepare you are preparing to fail."
Benjamin Franklin

"Success is where preparation and opportunity meet."
Bobby Unser

"To handle yourself, use your head; to handle others, use your heart."
Eleanor Roosevelt

"Leadership is about others."
Gloria L. Kelley

II

LEADERSHIP

1. Defining Leadership

When I was getting my MBA, a large part of what we studied was leadership. We were encouraged (make that 'required') to come up with our own definitions. The reason: Our professors wanted us to own the definition. They didn't want us to blindly adopt someone else's definition. Instead, since leadership is such an individual thing, they wanted us to be able to articulate our definition to others as well as to ourselves.

Ourselves? Yes, ourselves. Think about it. If you don't have a leadership style, you are liable to be like a lot of 'leaders' (wink, wink) who are friendly one day, gloomy the next, welcoming the next and angry the next. Team members don't know how to approach them. Often, in those kinds of environments, a familiar question rules the airwaves: "What kind of mood is the boss in today?" Sad. So sad.

Back to the definition. Here's mine: *Leadership is taking a person or persons from Point A to Point B, Point B being a place that they would not have sought or attained had it not been for the leader.* This says what the leader did, *not how* he or she accomplished it. Was the leader in the front of the pack? Maybe. Was the leader behind the pack? Maybe. How about part of the pack? Maybe that, too. Was the leader even around the pack? Could have been. Simply stated, there are many ways to lead.

For me, personally, *leadership is about empowering others to do what you know needs to get done.* I haven't yet come up with a 'picture' definition for this but I'm working on it. Meanwhile, I'll stick with the one above and add this one parenthetically. If you have suggestions, I welcome them.

2. Your 'Assignment'

Oh, okay, it's not an assignment; it's rather a strong suggestion. Prepare yourself to define leadership. Doing so will not only be enlightening for you but I can promise you that it will serve its purpose in working with your team members, your colleagues and other stakeholders. Only one suggestion for this: DO NOT memorize it. Instead, let it come out a little bit differently each time. Create a word picture of leadership, as I did when you 'saw' the person or persons going from Point A to Point B in my definition above. Make it a conversational definition, one that rolls off your tongue without forcing you to remember the exact right words and exact sequence of what you want to say.

If you would, please send me your definitions. I will post the most impactful ones on my Website with credit to you for providing it.

3. The Avalanche of Leadership Styles

Now that you have a solid definition of leadership in your mind (remember to make it visual), let's briefly discuss the many different ways in which leadership is portrayed. Depending on the guru, there are dozens of styles. Here are some:

Participative	Challenging	Investigative
Intensive	Cooperative	Empathic
Democratic	Tactical	Pacesetting
Collaborative	Consensus	Compassionate
Conventional	Teaching	Commanding
Servant	Exclusive	Innovative
Affiliative	Authoritative	Inclusive
Strategic	Coaching	Visionary
Dictatorial	Sympathetic	Didactic
Adaptive	Associative	Communicative

And, trust me, there are yet many others.

Question: Why are there this many and even more? Answer: Most authors want recognition. If they create a taxonomy (grouping) and it is adopted, then they will get the acclaim they wish. It doesn't really matter if they are calling something already defined by a different name. If we, the audience, use their nomenclature, then they get the acknowledgment they crave.

It is HIGHLY unlikely that you are going to select an existing leadership style from the list above (or any list) and have it fit you like a tailor-made suit. Instead, you should have your own leadership style, one to which you give thought and one that continues to evolve. In the next section, I am going to walk you through an exercise that will help you create a leadership style that speaks to *exactly* how you lead...or for those of you who are emerging leaders, how you *want* to lead.

Before we get into that, it is important that you see

some of the reasons for creating your own leadership style. Here are a few:

One of the things that people on your team want from you is consistency. They want and need to have confidence that how you lead today will be how you lead tomorrow. It is not productive for them to be wondering about this on a daily basis. If you explain to them your leadership style, you will sidestep lots of unproductive activity.

When you have a leadership style that is all your own, you can explain its elements. For example, if someone asks you what is the most important ingredient for a successful leader, you might answer integrity because integrity is at the heart of your leadership style. You won't have to search for a term because you will already have given it thought.

In yesterday's world, people interviewing for a job tended to be more…well, conservative. It was unlikely that they would ask you questions, other than the standard ones like: "What plans does the organization have regarding X, Y and Z?" In today's world, talented applicants want a good fit as much as you do. They will ask you some of the same questions that you will ask them. One of them likely will be something along the lines of: "What might I expect from you if I am on your team?" You need to be prepared to deliver something that shows them that you have given this thought. Your leadership style is just that something.

What about if you are interviewing for another position? Perhaps it is to be on a board of directors or a committee…or even another job within or outside of your current organization? In those instances, you can most certainly expect to be asked behavioral questions about how you lead. Being able to articulate how you lead will be a HUGE advantage in answering those making the inquiries.

And, as a leader, you are also expected to mentor and coach your team. Having them think about how they lead (especially peer to peer) is important. Modeling it for them is important. Having them go through a similar exercise will benefit everyone on the team.

4. My Leadership Style

Let me share my leadership style with you so that you can see what I mean. I don't claim it to be the best (I'm always striving to improve it) but it works for me. And I can't tell you how many times it has proven to be valuable.

I quickly sketch an illustration that represents my leadership. I do that because I want to confirm to my audience that this is not something I am delivering off the top of my head. When you see the illustration and its explanation, you will intuitively know that I'm not winging it. Note that I used the word 'quickly' to stress the fact that the illustration is but an anchor, not the focal point. Don't spend more than ten seconds on it. If I were sketching this on a white board, a flipchart or an 8½ x 11 piece of paper (or even on a napkin), it would take me less than five seconds to draw that star.

While I am sketching this, I am explaining why I chose it. "I chose to have a star represent my leadership style because stars, to me, represent excellence…as in hotel and restaurant ratings and the like."

Then I write the word ***integrity*** in the middle of the star and say "For me, at the core of leadership is integrity." I might add one or two additional sentences but it is essential that you not get on a soap box and preach. Simply explain your leadership style and let any explanations feed off of your audience's questions.

Then I write the word ***communication*** at one of the points on the star and offer one sentence on why I chose it. I do the same for four other words describing my leadership. Mine are ***collaboration, reliability, excellence*** and ***joy.*** As I explain each, it is my hope (and expectation) that the person or persons listening can begin to see a logical approach to leadership. By the time that I have finished, I can expect a few questions. Any dialogue that results is wonderful, including suggestions from them as to how I might further enhance it.

At the end, my illustration looks something like this:

Let me comment on the selection of 'joy' as one of the descriptors. There are differences between fun, happiness and joy. Fun is typically very momentary. Happiness is when pleasant things happen. Joy transcends that. Joy is fulfillment and can occur during wonderfully happy times or even during sad times. It happens when you know that you are doing the right things for the right reasons. For me, it is an important distinction.

5. YOUR Leadership Style

It is important for you to develop your own leadership style. Following is an exercise where you can do so. However, please remember that your leadership style is an ever-evolving descriptor, one that is dynamic, not static. Plan to work on it periodically.

Step 1

Let's get started. I am excited for you to complete this and have it available. When we finish, I will share with you several caveats to consider. First thing is for you to get a pad of paper. On one page, write as many words as you can (a minimum of 35) that speak to the leader that you are or wish to be. It's okay if some of them are similar but try your best to cover the waterfront. Also, limit the descriptors to one word. For example, instead of 'high quality' to describe the fact that you always aspire to produce the best possible product or service, use 'excellence' which, actually, is a more encompassing word. In my brief explanation of excellence, I include the high-quality issue. Stop here and create your list. Return when you are done.

Step 2

Now that you have your 'starter' list, choose a maximum of seven words that describe you. Don't select synonyms or even distant cousins. For example, reliability and dependability are similar. So are collaboration and teamwork. The wider the range, the more impressive is your leadership.

Step 3

Now pick an illustration to use. You are welcome to use the star that I chose or any other. The key thing is to be able to draw it in less than ten seconds. My art skills are limited but, as I am drawing a star, I talk about it so that the audience can easily recognize what I have drawn. Other things to draw might come from nature (a tree, a flower and the sun are good ones), from transportation (a car, a bicycle, a train, a plane or even a rocket ship), from sports (a soccer ball, a basketball court or a speedway), from shapes (a pentagon or a triangle), from structures (a ladder, a pyramid or a building) or from other items (a diamond, an arrow or a clock). As you are drawing it, you are explaining why you chose it and setting the table for the narrative on your leadership style.

Some Caveats

First, before you begin with the delivery, say something on the order of the following: "I have been working on how I lead (or may lead) for x number of years. I believe that I can articulate it but I ask you to remember that it has evolved over this period of time and will continue to do so."

Second, and very importantly, don't come across as a know it all. Providing your leadership style simply demonstrates that you are a student of leadership, that you are constantly working to improve your leadership and that you have invested in thinking about how those two interweave. Depending on the audience, you may want to solicit their input.

Third, as Shakespeare wrote, "brevity is the soul of wit." Nobody wants to listen to you pontificate. Briefly deliver your leadership style and, if there are any, respond to questions. In all likelihood, you will get some.

And, fourth, practice it. When opportunities avail themselves, you don't want to wish that you had armed yourself for that moment; then it's too late. Abraham Lincoln said: "I will prepare and, one day, my chance will come." Your leadership style should flow out of you easily and comfortably.

6. Two Notes
The Whole Package

If you are new to your team (or they to you), this is a perfect opportunity to share your approach to leadership with them. Doing so will give them occasion to ask questions, share concerns and understand where you are coming from. It is very comforting for team members to feel that the leader is a student of leadership.

Perhaps you are interviewing someone and he/she asks what to expect. Often this comes out as something like: "What's the culture like around here?" That is no time to stumble but, instead, to share your leadership style. You want the person sitting across from you to feel that there is a good fit between your style and their expectations. They won't know that unless you can provide them your side of the equation.

Or you could be on the other side of the table, interviewing for another position within the company (or even outside of it), maybe a board position or something of that nature. You will undoubtedly receive questions about how you lead. Unveiling your leadership style will go a long way to addressing any concerns.

Bits and Pieces

It is conceivable that you will receive a question like:

"What do you think is the most important quality that a leader must have?" It may come in various forms but it will usually tie to something like that. Here you have two opportunities.

First, since you have given it some thought, you can easily pull what you feel to be the most important characteristic from your illustration. I would answer "Integrity" and then explain why. I can do so because I had already given it considerable thought when I created my leadership style.

Second, you can bridge to the full explanation with something like: "It's interesting that you should ask that because I have been studying leadership and developing my own leadership style. The short answer to your question is 'Integrity' but, if you will give me but two minutes, I would like to share with you a more complete answer." What a terrific segue for you. Not only will you be providing a more complete answer but you will also show what a good opportunist and presenter you are.

7. Followership

I would be remiss if I didn't mention something about followership. Before commenting on it, it is important to remind you of its evolution. For most of humankind's existence, being a follower pretty much meant waiting for orders from above and then fulfilling them…what we know to be a command-and-control environment. That worked fine with one problem: There was no input from those on the team. Everything was based on what the leader (commander, president, executive-in-charge) decided. Although the too many cooks spoil the broth approach was justification, it didn't usually trump something like what C. S. Lewis wrote: "Two heads are better than one, not because either is infallible, but because they are unlikely to go wrong in the same direction."

Progressive followership involves all team members. Leaders now solicit new ideas, alternate approaches, warnings and constructive feedback from the team. One is applauded for speaking up, not chastised. This needs to be done within a working framework. In other words, the boss invites input but, when the decision is made, it is time for each team member to carry it out. There is a time for planning and a time for doing. When the team gets into the doing stage, it is time to stop the pushback…save for something critical arising, of course.

Servant Leadership is an increasingly popular culture, one that is demonstrating remarkable results for the organizations that adopt it. [Organizations utilizing it *significantly* outperform organizations that stick with a top-down culture.] At the heart of this culture is progressive followership.

There is much more to be found about servant leadership. We will touch on some of it a bit later. However, a further study on it will be of value to you and to your organization. You might begin with the Robert K. Greenleaf Center for Servant Leadership *(www.greenleaf.org/what-is-servant-leadership)* or any of a myriad of books on the subject.

KEY POINTS

1. Have a solid definition of leadership, one that you can succinctly share with others.

2. Instead of pulling something 'off the shelf,' develop a visual explanation of your own leadership style. Keep practicing and refining it.

3. Create an atmosphere of progressive followership.

4. Do some reading to better understand servant leadership.

"Before you are a leader, success is all about growing yourself. When you become a leader, success is all about growing others."
Jack Welch

"There is a difference between listening and waiting for your turn to speak."
Simon Sinek

"Tthe speed of the leader determines the rate of the pack."
Wayne Lukas

"Everyone should be quick to listen, slow to speak and slow to become angry."
James 1:19

"I've learned that people will forget what you said, people will forget what you did, but people will never forget how you made them feel."
Maya Angelou

"Great leaders are great listeners. This enriches the team AND the team members by benefiting from everyone's input."
Gloria L. Kelley

III
LEADERSHIP TOOLS

1. Nature or Nurture?

Quite a bit has been written about whether good leaders are born or made. Does one person have the innate ability to lead while another does not? Can we turn anyone into a successful leader simply by teaching them the right things to do? Or is it a combination of the two?

At one point in time, it was fully believed that leadership was something akin to having a leadership gene. If you came from the right family, you had this gene and could lead. If not, then your lot in life was simply to take and follow orders. That's at least part of the reason why kings passed their thrones down to their heirs, typically the oldest male. [The people did not often dispute this, possibly because they valued having their heads remaining connected to their necks.]

But when royalty became more figurative than literal, it gave birth to determining why some people could lead and some could not. Although the journey is a bit more complicated, the first step was the belief that leaders had particular gifts. Thus, if you wanted to find a great leader, you needed to find someone who possessed all, or at least most, of these traits. One of the problems with this approach was that there was no universal agreement as to which traits made up the set. How important was eloquence? Where did looks fit in, if even they did? Was faith a key component? How about analytical skills? And what about morality? I trust that you can see the dilemma.

The current consensus agreement is that nature and nurture combine to deliver successful leaders. Given someone with solid mental faculties and an appropriate demeanor, a leader could be fashioned through training. The nature versus nurture debate remains alive and well but it is not something we will address here. [There is much, especially academic, literature available, should you be so interested.] Suffice it to say that leadership is a combination of what you were inherently provided and what you developed.

2. Art or Science?

Another lively discussion involves whether great leaders lean on their own instincts or upon more quantitative tools. In this instance, again, virtually everyone agrees that both are required. What is in dispute is the balance between the two. I won't get into the middle of this debate but I will offer one thing: Aspiring leaders who do not draw heavily from both will find their ambitions short lived, to say the least. In short, it is an art versus science debate.

The art or intuitive side is relatively obvious. It answers the question: "What is your gut telling you to do?" Instinct must be a factor in any decision-making process. But the Bible reminds us: "Yet these people slander whatever they do not understand, and the very things they do understand by *instinct*, as irrational animals do, will destroy them." [Jude 1:10]

The science side is not so evident. It is the use of tools to help leaders consider solutions (for challenges as well as opportunities), to chart courses towards those solutions, to evaluate performance and to loop through the cycle, if necessary and possible. Right now, tools are flying off the bookshelves...literally. Virtually every leadership book these days stresses the importance of utilizing leadership tools. These range from ones long in existence (cash flow and other number based reports) to brand new ones, a few of which I will introduce here.

One request. If you have tools that you believe this readership would benefit in seeing, please send them to my Website. I will post the best tools.

3. Leadership Tool Belt

In my MBA Program, a concept was introduced that I have continued to use. It is called the Leadership Tool Belt and it is a way of capturing and organizing a wide variety of tools that will benefit you as a leader. It requires just a little bit of imagination.

Envision a carpenter's tool belt. You know the canvas one I am talking about. It has places to hold a hammer, screwdrivers, a wrench and other tools so that you don't have to go to your toolbox every thirty seconds to retrieve a different or additional tool that you will likely be using with some frequency. The tool belt also has pouches to hold nails, brads, screws and so forth...for exactly the same reason (i.e., lessening the wasted interval of accessing them each time). Okay, good.

This is an imaginary tool belt, one that you can design in any manner you wish. I want you to remove all the tool holders, leaving only the pouches. Remember, this is imaginary. Now I want you to envision maybe ten pouches on this belt. You can add others as you think them appropriate. Each pouch will hold a distinct set of tools, in this case *leadership* tools. Let's take a look at some of the pouches with a short explanation of each:

> ***Idea Generation*** – These tools enable you to maximize creativity, especially from your team. When you are in the mode of coming up with ideas (e.g., features for a product or new markets to enter), you want to generate as many good ideas as possible. These tools help you do so.

> ***Priority Setting*** – We rarely have enough resources, especially time, money and personnel, to do everything on our to-do list. In a business setting, spending time on the wrong things is entirely wasteful. These tools help you decide which projects to undertake and in what priority.

> ***Time Management*** – Most people would agree that they do not efficiently (and effectively) take advantage of the time allocated to them. These tools help you and team members do so.

> ***Meetings Management*** – One of the greatest waste of time in an organization is an inefficient meeting. It can needlessly consume time, not be tremendously productive and, in fact, create more frustration than value. There are a number of tools that can differentiate you from someone who does not break out of this wasteful mode.

> ***Change Management*** – John Kennedy said: "Everything changes but change itself." How right

he was. Most leaders have no or limited ways to address this. How wonderful it would be if you could map out an approach to a change initiative. There are many tools that can help you do so.

Strategic Management – Unless living in a cave, leaders understand the need to think long term. However, most do not maximize ways to do so. These tools allow you to have a more systematic approach to strategic thinking.

Crisis Management – There is a centuries-old saying not attributed to any particular individual: "Forewarned is forearmed" (the Latin being "'praemonitus, praemunitus"). Too many organizations deal with issues when they arise instead of investing time anticipating them. There are loads of tools that can help you do this without consuming gobs of time.

Others – The list can go on and on: Human resource management, project management and so forth.

You can label them however you wish. You can have as many as you wish. And you can put them in any order that you wish. The idea is to have separate pouches, *each with multiple tools.* Then, when the time calls for it, you can draw out the right one for the right circumstance.

4. Two Examples
Rotational Brainstorming

Let's select a tool from the Idea Generation pouch. Most people are familiar with brainstorming. Let's say that you want to come up with additional features for a product or service. Your team, sitting before a flipchart, tosses out ideas as they think of them. At the end, you come up with a list of ideas BUT, and here's the kicker, you likely don't get the most out of that brainstorming session. The reason: Contributions were unbalanced. For one thing, as in most such sessions, one or two people dominate. That could be for any of a number of reasons, including the need to be heard. For another, also as in most such sessions, one or two people will lay back, perhaps not wanting to offer something that could be ridiculed or just because they are not comfortable being more proactive. As for the rest, *if* they think of something (the key word being *'if'*), they will offer something. Otherwise, they will partially listen and partially think of other things. This less-than-perfect process is called traditional brainstorming.

Now let's look at an excellent idea generation tool. It is called rotational brainstorming. In this situation, your goal remains exactly the same, to come up with additional features for a product or service. However, the process is considerably different. Instead of a contribute if you feel like it atmosphere, the facilitator goes around the room asking each person, in turn, if they have anything to offer. If so, they make their contribution. If not, they simply say 'pass' and the opportunity moves to the next person.

Here are the results: The person who loves to hear himself or herself talk (whom I like to call the motormouth), is limited to one chance each time around the group. The person who says 'pass' (the wallflower) will eventually, due to self-conceived peer pressure, begin making contributions. And the others will have to stay involved because they don't want to appear uninvolved when their turn comes up. You haven't created any friction with the motormouth ("Come on, let someone else offer something."); you haven't embarrassed the wallflower ("Don't you have *anything* to offer?); and you have kept the entire team engaged. In addition, you've provided some variety. Instead of "Oh, no, here goes the boss again with his one-trick pony," your team will show some interest and enjoy change ups to the idea generation process.

One caveat: For rotational brainstorming, your team can't be too large. Otherwise it takes too long to complete each cycle. Eight or so participants is pretty much the ceiling. Overall, your demonstrating effective variety will be well appreciated. I don't know how many times someone from my team has thanked me for introducing them to a tool that they used in other scenarios.

Affinity Grouping

This is a combination tool, part Idea Generation and part Priority Setting. It is a two stage exercise. Once an objective has been set (e.g., adding features to a product or service), a clear purpose statement is written and made visible to everyone participating. Then each attendee takes a number of 3" x 3" Post-It Notes, perhaps twenty such sheets. There is no discussion during this first stage. On each one sheet, the participant writes a single idea that he or she believes would be a good idea. [Encourage them to be very brief in what they write.] The participant then takes that note and posts it to a flipchart (or a white board or wall) in no particular order. Then the participant returns to write a second idea and so forth. Meanwhile, all the other contributors are doing the same thing. After an appropriate amount of time, usually when the postings slow down, the facilitator stops this first stage. By this time, the flipchart is typically well covered with individual Post-It Notes.

For the second stage, one or two participants are tasked

with grouping the individual ideas. Typically, four or five such groups emerge, often one entitled 'Miscellaneous.' When that is completed, a single idea is summarized from each group. Now all the participants can discuss these groups and determine which have optimal credibility and what courses of action to follow, in effect prioritizing which should be explored and in what order.

Bottom Line

These two tools are simple but effective ones. The point to be made here is that there are literally hundreds (if not thousands) of tools in all of the categories (and others) mentioned above. The progressive leader determines which tools will maximize the experience that the team (or he/she alone) is facing. If you have not collected tools, you will keep doing the same thing over and over again, ad nauseam. If you have tools from which to choose, your team will look forward to learning them and looking at challenges through very different lenses.

I was tempted to include more tools. However, after considering this, I realized that doing so is not the point of this book. When it comes to leadership tools, the point that I want to make is that you need to be proactive in accumulating and organizing them, thus having them available for you when the appropriate time arises.

My plan is to post a good number of these tools on my Website. I invite you to submit ones that you believe should be included. You will then be able to retrieve and employ them. In effect, the Website will serve as your Leadership Tool Belt. But, at the same time, I suggest that you still keep your own list…with brief descriptors to remind you how to employ each tool.

KEY POINTS

1. Leaders possess both innate and learned abilities. Great leaders draw from both.

2. Leaders can go on either feel or science. The former is intuitive. The latter is analytical. Great leaders utilize both.

3. A Leadership Tool Belt encourages leaders to accumulate tools that will help them and their teams maximize performance in different circumstances. Great leaders gather tools and wisely utilize ones that provide optimal value and variety.

4. Visit and contribute to my Website *(www.glorialkelley.com)* to see an ever growing list of tools.

"Train people well enough so they can leave. Treat them well enough so they don't want to."
Richard Branson

"A boss has the title; a leader has the people."
Simon Sinek

"The best way to find yourself is to lose yourself in the service of others."
Mahatma Gandhi

"Volunteers don't get paid, not because they're worthless, but because they're priceless."
Sherry Anderson

"A successful lawsuit is the one worn by a policeman."
Robert Frost

"Every unfortunate event does not give rise to a lawsuit."
Judge Mills Lane

"Once you understand that the power of your position has little, if anything, to do with success, you can begin to coach, mentor and assist your team by empowering and supporting their needs and progress."
Gloria L. Kelley

IV
YOUR TEAM

In his book <u>Good to Great</u>, Jim Collins places great emphasis on the employment process. In a nutshell, it involves a three-step process: (1) Hire the right people; (2) maximize their potential; and (3) remove the wrong people. Of course, it's not as easy as that sounds, not a plug and play progression. Instead, it is quite a complex process. Although we will touch on each of these, I strongly recommend that you read the book. It is a must-have addition to your library, as is his sequel <u>Great by Choice</u>.

1. Hiring

Some organizations don't like to rely on anything other than applications, resumes and interviews in hiring full and part-time employees. If it 'feels' right, they go with their gut. After personally experiencing some trial and error in this regard, I believe that there are significant tools that can help one achieve a higher rate of success.

At CASA Kane County, we use a particular behavioral assessment instrument that we have found to be exceptional. It is called the Devine Inventory. It measures 33 behaviors and relates them to specific job descriptions. With it, we have had immense success in hiring the right people, something that seemed so challenging just a few years earlier.

You may or may not choose to explore this. Obviously, it is up to you. If you are interested and cannot discover it otherwise, contact me at my website and I will put you in touch with the company that administers and helps interpret it.

The right word is 'fit.' If you want a productive team member, his/her goals must be as important to you as your organization's goals. Those organizations that simply look to see if the potential employee can provide the skills needed are making a huge mistake. Yes, what that individual brings to the table is important, truly essential. However, if there isn't a two-way exchange of value, the relationship won't last. Bottom line: Make *absolutely* certain that your organization can provide what that individual needs. Financial compensation is, of course, a key component. But there are other things, too: Work/life balance, growth opportunities, physical setting, benefits, freedom, fulfillment and so forth.

In other words, be as diligent in discovering what you can do for the candidate as you are in what he/she can do for you.

2. Assigning

In a fantasy organization, everyone is where they can perform at their best and love what they are doing. Guess what? It's not like that. Although many organizations may get pretty close to this idyllic state, there is always work to do in this area. [That is why the Devine Inventory that we use is so important…and so helpful.]

There are several essential reasons not to assume that everyone is where they belong. For one thing, situations change. Maybe the job description is no longer of value in the way it is written. If the employee is comfortable with that description and then it changes, discomfort (or worse) can rear its ugly head. After all, resistance to change is inherent in us all, especially when it comes in a form that threatens one's basic needs. [See Abraham Maslow's Hierarchy of Needs for more on this. It's very interesting.]

For another, perhaps the interests or capabilities of the employee change. Maybe they complete an academic or training program and feel that they deserve to be doing something else. Maybe their family life changes and they can offer more or less of their time and attention. Maybe someone in a more critical function left and this is the only person who can best pick it up before there is negative impact to the organization.

There are three things that comprise placing the right person in the right job:

1. *What does the organization need?*

   It is a rare instance when a candidate proposes some skill that he/she possesses that you haven't already discovered and you now revamp the job description to include it.

2. *What can the individual provide?*

   You learn this through paperwork, references and interviews. When possible, which it is most of the time, focus on metrics. What can be measured to demonstrate this applicant's existing and potential skill set?

3. ***What does the individual want?***

Although understanding what the individual wants is essential, be careful in believing that what is put on the table is a take it or leave it condition. Instead, more than likely, they might be throwing out supposed requirements only to have something to fall back on during negotiation. Alternatively, they may have some short-term distractions that could get in the way of their objectivity. Two examples: (1) Wanting a position because it offers more money, more benefits, more prestige, etc.; and (2) believing that they are ready to handle a challenging position beyond their skill set. Concerning the latter, a great majority of people think more highly of their skill set than is warranted. You, and those you empower to help make good assignments, need to be very cognizant of this.

3. Terminating

Whether you call it downsizing, rightsizing, scaling, reducing, economizing or terminating, *it's still letting people go*. [By the way, be very careful about your use of these or any other synonyms. Many, maybe most, people get very put off by them.] For me, terminating someone' is the most difficult part of my job.

However, when someone you either inherit or even hire does not belong for any of a myriad of justifiable reasons, you need to let them go. Naturally, this decision comes well after you have made every effort to realign them with their responsibilities, both functional and behavioral.

Unless you are terminating a function and this results in having to release employees, there are generally two types of people who need to be let go: Those who are a malignancy to the organization and those who just don't fit in or are not performing. Ridding the organization of the former is clear and often results in a Whew! kind of sensation. Among other things, your focus needs to be on protecting yourself legally. Releasing the latter is much more difficult.

In my twenty plus years of working with people, I have come across a number of individuals who have had big hearts but were just not the right fit for the position and/ or the culture. It's not that they were bad people (by any extent), just that you need people on your team who will embrace the mission while capitalizing on collaboration opportunities with colleagues (managers, peers, team members and volunteers). This learning opportunity for me, especially during my early years, was very difficult.

Once you reach the decision that it is best for the organization that they no longer be associated with it, how you frame this in communicating it to the individual will go a very long way to demonstrating to others (and yourself) what kind of leader you are. I have seen too many leaders move towards an adversarial relationship with the employee and the ending has not been pretty. Often, in fact, lawsuits result. This needn't happen, if you keep the interests of the soon to be terminated employee in mind.

Of course, the best way to minimize the likelihood of this happening is to have clear procedures and communication in place from day one. This would include one month, three month, six month and one year evaluations. By the way, I suggest at least a one month probationary period, preferably three months. What you want to do is identify problems early on in the process to be able to avoid them later.

When it's time to part company, you are seeking the best outcome for the organization AND for the individual. [It's when the latter is disregarded that problems arise.] When I have to terminate someone, I always frame it as a misfit, not their fault and not ours. Once setting the table, I tell them that I want to help them find another position, one that better suits them. They now have a choice: Do they want my help or does their disappointment/anger negatively consume the next steps? If they want my help, I will either make an effort to work with them or provide them with the benefits of an employment service. What I do depends on a number of factors, including my availability and funding.

One bit of caution. You may have attorneys on staff, as do I. However, don't rely on them to handle the legal issues related to employment. For one thing, they probably don't have the time. For another, it is not likely that they have expertise in this field. If you become involved in a contentious termination and you need legal representation, secure it from outside your organization.

One other thing: If you need to terminate someone, you simply need to do it. This is especially true if it is obvious to others on your team. One essential characteristic of leadership is backbone. Sometimes, great leaders have to choose when not to do something. This is not one such case; you must act decidedly. Your team members are looking closely at whether or not you take action. Failure to do so will more than disappoint them.

Someone I respect told me about a situation he faced a number of years ago. He led a department of twelve, one of whom was clearly a problem. He kept trying to realign this employee but to no avail. His team encouraged him to terminate this person but he refused, coming up with a myriad of excuses for not doing so. More reasons accumulated but still no action. Then his second in command marched into his office, wrote the word 'wimp' on his whiteboard and walked out, not uttering a word. Immediately thereafter, he initiated action, only wishing that he had done so earlier.

When I was in graduate school, I remember people discussing the 3 P's. When I researched them, I came across a half dozen such trilogies. After a while, my head was spinning with P words: process, prediction, policies, product, profit, purpose and so forth. One thing that I noticed was that each set either began with or included 'People'. Without the right people in the right places doing the right things, you are doomed to underachieve or worse.

KEY POINTS

1. In your hiring process, consider using behavioral assessment instruments. Intuition can often misdirect you.

2. When hiring someone, make certain that the organization's needs as well as the individual's needs are both met.

3. Don't ignore the fact that functions change and people change, not necessarily in the same direction.

4. If the time arrives when you need to terminate someone, suck it up and get it done. Not doing so promises more woe than it is worth.

5. When needing to terminate someone, make certain that you have all your legal i's dotted and t's crossed. Doing so will avoid, or at least minimize, unnecessary complications.

6. Do not use your internal legal services to handle human resource lawsuits. They have neither the time nor the expertise to work on them.

7. If you need to terminate someone, offer to help them find another position. If you cannot justify a recommendation, offer to provide them a confirmation of employment.

*"The board's role is to pull management
out of the trees to see the forest."*
Pearl Zhu

*"New board members need to be informed about
what is expected of them. If they don't know what is
expected, they might create their own expectations....
and some of them I might not like."*
Theodore Blair Flickinger

*"Knowing is not enough; we must apply.
Willing is not enough; we must do."*
Johann Wolfgang von Goethe

*"Do more than belong: Participate. Do more
than care: Help. Do more than believe: Practice.
Do more than be fair: Be kind. Do more than
forgive: Forget. Do more than dream: Work."*
William Arthur Ward

*"Board members play a remarkably essential
role in helping set the direction for an organization.
Do not succumb to making it an honorary position.
If you do that, you will miss out on a critical
contribution to your success."*
Gloria L. Kelley

V

YOUR BOARD

I have found there to be enormous disparity when it comes to how organizations view the role of their boards. It ranges from 'essential' on the left to 'ceremonial' on the right. I am of the position that the needle needs to hover dramatically to the left. For those who believe that board membership is a gratuity for individuals to whom one owes a favor, rethink your logic. If that's what you have, you will spend considerable unproductive time with them and not attain the incredible value that the board can provide. I cannot emphasize this enough.

Boards

Not everyone calls its board a board of directors. There are loads of popular names for it, including executive board, directorate, board of governors, board of trustees, administrative board, governing board, governing council and many others. I like board of directors because it clearly suggests the function (i.e., 'direct'). Nevertheless, I wouldn't get too hung up on this. If you already have a title for those serving this function and it doesn't cause problems, then stick with it. Your actions need to have purpose. What is of paramount purpose is that everyone uses the same terminology. [As an aside, I advocate your having an organization specific lexicon available to all your team members. This could avoid unnecessary confusion going forward.]

I wrote a piece on boards. It's in the appendix entitled "Ten for Greatness: Board Member Characteristics." It might be valuable for you to look it over.

Important Note

There is one VERY important point that I want to make. When I finally fully grasped and implemented this, it made a world of difference. There are two levels of responsibility in an organization, vision and execution. Although there is a small amount of overlap, vision is the responsibility of the executive director on up through the board. Execution is the responsibility of the executive director down through the team. If you let board members tinker with the operations of the organization, you are asking for a world of trouble. When this happens, board members often send mixed (maybe opposite) signals to what you are striving to achieve, may confuse your team members because of accountability issues and frequently do not have the skill set to make suggestions in areas they invade in spite of thinking that they both understand the operational level and "know just what the team needs." Further, allowing this to take place seriously undermines your leadership. It's not that you want to 'protect' your domain. Instead, you want *suggestions* from the board. But YOU need to be the conduit and the one implementing them if, indeed, they are worthy.

Think of the split as being like this: *With you*, the board decides ***where*** the ship is going. *With you*, the team decides ***how*** to get there. [When you study the many differences between a leader and a manager, you will see this as being one of the notable distinctions.] If you want to maximize your organization's performance, maintain this separation. The board assures that the right things are done and the executive director assures that they are done right.

One caveat: Rules are made to have exceptions. The separation of board members and team members is important, nay even vital. BUT there are times when a board member has the particular skills (and bandwidth to employ them) that are needed for a specific circumstance. Naturally, in those situations, we will invite the board member to do so.

Board Makeup

How many people should be on your board? I smile when I am asked this question. It's like someone asking how many slides they should have for a presentation. The answer to both questions is the same: It depends. For board size, it depends on such factors as legal requirements, size of the organization, complexity of the organization and functions needing to be covered. There is no cookie cutter answer to this. Further, you may want to change your bylaws if you find that whatever number you have initially chosen is too large or too small.

My belief is that each member of the board has to be

- committed to the organization's vision and mission;
- extremely talented, especially in his/her field of expertise;

- willing to invest time and effort to keep the organization striving to attain ever growing standards of excellence;

- willing to invest financial resources in the organization;

- willing to use his/her networking abilities;

- willing to understand and participate in all fiduciary duties internally and externally to protect the organization; and

- willing to think about the organization outside of 'official' board meeting times.

The board has a fiduciary responsibility as leaders of the organization. How they handle that responsibility speaks volumes to their commitment. On our board, each member gives generously of their time, talents, connections and treasures. I like to say that, among other things, board members need to have influence *and* affluence. Those are no small parts of their contributions to the organization.

Diversity

When it comes to diversity, this is not a concern that should be taken lightly. Generally, I think that a good guideline is to have the board reflect the constituency that the organization addresses. However, this is not always possible for a myriad of reasons. Gender, race, religion, age and other classifications do not always lend themselves to defining your board's makeup. For example, CASA Kane County focuses on abused and neglected youths. We are very intentional in getting input from our target audience (staff, volunteers and community) but it would not be appropriate for us to involve them proportionately in board decisions. For one thing, they will not have the maturity to understand such things as endowments, project management and the like. Boards are not teaching occasions; they are action opportunities. Besides that, many people do not have the time, interest or skills to contribute to the workings of the board. I will not be satisfied unless everyone is able to grab an oar and row as a unit.

CASA Kane County has 25 well qualified and engaged board members. Each is a cherished and valuable participant. By the way, with yourself included, you would be wise to have an odd number of board members. Although it is not likely to happen, at least very often, you don't want to reach a stalemate that you cannot resolve. At the very least, make certain that you have a procedure for breaking any tie.

As for whether or not you have the right board members, here's the litmus test: If your board members have relevant skills, invest themselves in the organization and don't care about personal acclaim, then you have the right members. It is also imperative that they know their roles and responsibilities. They need to provide oversight without succumbing to micromanaging tendencies. If the executive director is successfully minimizing the overlap between board members and staff/volunteers, then execution will be at its best.

Selecting Board Members

For CASA Kane County, board members come from a variety of sources. First and foremost, we look for leaders from our primary committee, the Chairman's Advisory Panel (CAP). These are individuals who have been the bridge between the board's strategy and the team's execution. They have a good appreciation for both.

However, we are not locked into a sequence. If we determine that long-term and strong donors with solid business backgrounds are a possibility, we will approach them with consideration. Additionally, there might be community-minded individuals that board members are recommending. A few months before our annual May elections, individuals are reviewed along with the current term limits and board composition to review gaps and determine needs based on the board's roles and responsibilities.

And there is one other thing: We don't just willy-nilly 'think' that someone might make a good board member. There is a substantial selection process that includes history, testing and multiple interviews. Only when everyone on the board is satisfied will an offer be extended.

Board Terms

One of your challenges will be determining how long a board member should serve. This should be included in your bylaws. Don't fall into the trap of letting someone serve too long. Although it is tempting because of his/her past, current and likely future contributions, I will give you two reasons not to allow that to happen.

First, the board needs fresh blood. No, not that kind of blood…new ideas. It is too easy for board members to comfortably settle into 'ways that are working' and not look for ways to do something better. As Jim Collins wrote: "Good is the enemy of great." Don't settle for an eight when a nine or ten is within reach.

Second, very importantly, board members need time to refresh and recharge. Once they have served their terms, they need and deserve a sabbatical. Whether or not they return to the board after a break, they will likely be able to offer you new ideas because they are looking at the organization from a slightly different perspective.

Which brings me to one more thing. Stay in touch with former board members. Value them and let them know that you do. Aside from the selfish reason of wanting to benefit from their ongoing ideas and support, they deserve to feel the joy and honor of how the organization is doing…and knowing that they contributed to the forward progress.

Basic Functions

So, what are you looking for when you put together or reconfigure a board? There are two schools of thought here and they mimic the two schools of thought that are followed by NFL coaches during their drafts. One school says that if you find someone especially good, ask that person to be on your board. You can find a place for an individual like that. The other school says to determine your needs and then proactively try to fill them. Although I tend to lean towards the former, I still leave room for the latter. Quite frankly, I'd rather have multiple layers of expertise than miss out on occasion to add someone really good to my board.

Generally, I determine what business functions are indispensable for a board to possess. In most instances, they include (in alphabetic order)…

- accounting;
- business;
- finance;
- fundraising;

- grant writing;
- human resources;
- insurance;
- inventory management;
- law;
- manufacturing and/or distribution (depending on what your non-profit does);
- marketing; and
- technology.

You may have others but these are generally the core. Again, I want to remind you to keep the board at the visionary level and not let them get into the operational weeds.

In the case of CASA Kane County, our having duplicates for these core functions allows us to more effectively utilize our board members on committees. [We will address committees and the like in the next chapter.] For example, we need marketing expertise for a number of our functions, including various fundraising events (our gala, golf outing and other events). It would be too much of an imposition to ask one board member to work on multiple committees. Our having overlapping expertise allows us to sidestep that dilemma. Working with committees also provides a better overview and experience to collaborate and get the best product.

On the other hand, the last thing that you want is to have a board member feel as though he/she is an extra wheel. You need to find meaningful contribution opportunities for each board member, lest their interest wane and they look at the board membership as an obligation rather than as an important cause.

Don't Forget!

It would be a shame for you or anyone on your team to forget that board members are volunteers. They don't have to be doing this. They don't have to be contributing their time, talent and treasures to your organization. There are lots of other things that they could be doing. As you know, there are many non-profit entities wishing that they could get board members who could provide exceptional value to their organization. In many ways, it's like a marriage. If you take your partner for granted, soon that partner will disengage, informally or formally.

I suggest that the best ways to avoid estrangement include the following:

- Share your clear expectations of them;

- Show your appreciation of them;

- Involve them with meaningful issues;

- Listen to them (although that does not mean you have to agree with them);

- Always remind them of the mission (not to the point of pestering);

- Keep the saying 'no money, no mission' alive and well;

- Be respectful of their time (for example, keep meetings to the time you promised and not a minute longer);

- Ensure there are no surprises through the five pillars of advocacy, people, processes, technology and finance; and

- Stay in touch with them (but not so much as to become an annoyance).

Rules for the Board

Robert's Rules of Order should be in play when your board meets. But don't get caught up in its formality. Being correct in procedure while being wrong in outcome is a sad result. You may want to create some guidelines for the board to consider rather than having them become experts in the formal procedures. If you do create guidelines, make them specific to your organization. And, of course, get member feedback on drafts before putting these guidelines into play.

KEY POINTS

1. Whatever you call your board of directors, have it be the title that everyone uses.

2. The board focuses on *where* the organization is headed while the team focuses on *how* to get there.

3. Be careful how you balance size and functionality on your board. Too large and you may lose involvement. Too small and you may not be able to adequately cover functions.

4. Identify qualifications you are looking for concerning board members.

5. Diversity is important but not just for diversity's sake. Have it make sense.

6. Be certain to carefully assess potential board members. This cannot simply be a popularity contest or part of a spoils system.

7. Always be thinking about how to keep your board members engaged. Don't have their being on the board simply something that they add to their bio.

8. Make certain to identify and cover all the functions that are essential to the board's effectiveness.

9. A set of guidelines for your board to use could be a wise investment of your time rather than having the members try to develop expertise with <u>Robert's Rules of Order</u>.

10. And don't forget that they are volunteers, serving on the board for all the right and righteous reasons.

"A committee is a group of the unprepared, appointed by the unwilling to do the unnecessary."
Fred Allen

"A committee is a group of people who individually can do nothing, but who, as a group, can meet and decide that nothing can be done."
Fred Allen

"I'm not thinking about anything when I'm climbing, which is part of the appeal. I'm focused on executing what's in front of me."
Alex Honnold

"Happiness does not come from doing easy work but from the afterglow of satisfaction that comes after the achievement of a difficult task that demanded our best."
Theodore Isaac Rubin

"Change is inevitable. If you're not changing, then you're being left behind."
Gloria L. Kelley

VI

YOUR COMMITTEES

I laugh at those first two quotes from Fred Allen above because I know that, without our committees, we would not have had the kind of success that we have achieved. The right committees contribute to focus, joy and the importance of change. Let's discuss these. The following is a Wikipedia definition. Although a bit tedious, it is actually quite good.

A committee is a body of one or more persons that is subordinate to a deliberative assembly. Usually, the assembly sends matters into a committee as a way to explore them more fully than would be possible if the assembly itself were considering them. Committees may have different functions and their type of work differs depending on the type of the organization and its needs.

Committees are incredibly important. I'm not solely talking about board committees (although those are vital) but also about sub-groupings of any assembly of individuals. For example, CASA Kane County has an advisory committee called the Chairman's Advisory Panel or CAP. We will discuss it and other committees in this chapter.

Maximizing Use of Your Board

I suspect that your board members are or were successful in their professional careers. It is likely that many are still working, either doing what helped them achieve that success or pursuing a second career. Others might have retired. Unequivocally, no matter where they are in their career spectrum, each is a doer. They get things done.

As an aside, a couple of decades ago, all the rage in leadership books was planning, both strategic and tactical. Book after book, seminar after seminar, training program after training program came out with ways for organizations to maximize their planning effectiveness and efficiency. Then along came process improvement. [You might remember Six Sigma as a leading credential in this field.] And, finally, the emphasis shifted to execution: *How* does one take this analysis and planning into action?

Board members are typically get it done people. But they may not have the time to address individual initiatives that need to be moved along the proverbial conveyor belt. Very importantly, you don't want them constructing the building, only serving as its architect. The best way that they can do this is by serving on specific committees, especially those involving fundraising. The diversity of the board and other committees needs to be analyzed and reviewed often in order to capture the needed strengths of filling the gaps for the organization.

Board Committees

In our organization, we have five primary board committees:

1. Executive & Board Development
2. Finance & Legal
3. Advancement & Sponsorship

4. Marketing & Outreach

5. Audit and Compliance

Each board member serves on one of these committees. Your major committees may be the same or different. What matters is that they cover the waterfront. You're much better having overlap between committees than risking a gap that goes unattended.

You might have noticed in reviewing these five committees that there is not one specifically devoted to legacy/endowments, a critically important pursuit if you are intending to weather economic storms and have the wherewithal to pursue new major initiatives. That's because everyone on our board participates on this committee in some capacity. Their doing so allows you to open new doors and opportunities. As a result, we have made quite remarkable strides in building our endowment from a token amount to something substantial. And we are ever looking to take it to the next, next and next levels, as we have done thus far.

When we first started to strategize about an endowment campaign, even our modest ambitions seemed almost out of reach. Instead of telling ourselves how difficult this would be, we simply determined to eat the elephant one bite at a time. We did some planning and then went after it. We put together some literature to help.

When it comes to our board, participation on committees has been the catalyst to achieve so very much. Just as a football team has different units (offense, defense and special teams), the board committees come together to form a winning combination. Because of their caring hearts and big-picture perspective, they lead this important initiative in perpetuity.

Chairman's Advisory Panel (CAP)

The CAP is a committee made up of individuals who want to give back to their community. Many of them have board credentials. In fact, when a board vacancy occurs, CAP members are the first ones considered.

The CAP meets quarterly, whereas the board meets bimonthly (i.e., four versus six times per year). CAP members serve as CASA ambassadors in the community and become actively involved in special events. For example, we have an annual event called the Super Heroes Luncheon. At a recent event, nearly 600 guests heard a powerful testimony on how one man overcame enormous life challenges. He was able to beat the odds because one person in his life believed that he could do the impossible. In our case, we are proud to have nearly 250 dedicated and caring CASA/GAL volunteers who create consistency for abused and neglected children to thrive. There is no question that the foster care system is overburdened. Our advocates work tirelessly to make sure that the children we serve are made to feel special and loved. CAP members, along with generous sponsors, make that event, and several others, successfully happen.

Community Connections Committee

We recently revitalized and created a new structure, one that we determined would be of significant value. Its primary purpose, as the name suggests, is to determine which activities have the greatest potency in spreading awareness of CASA. Members determine to whom we should reach out, especially social service agencies, businesses and, of course, any organization working on behalf of children. They further determine if education, recruitment efforts, special events, special campaigns or other activities provide the greatest bang for the buck. Since we don't have unlimited fiscal or personnel resources, this committee helps us focus on how assets should be allocated.

Structuring Your Volunteer Community

Our overarching belief is that "Everyone can do something." Committees are a meaningful avenue for that to happen. Some volunteers have limited time and resources. That's fine. We appreciate their working on one event, maybe if only to help create literature, set up or just greet guests. Others have more to offer and we welcome their being able to do so. Anywhere along the range, though, we seek to make them see how important their contribution is to the overall achievement of our objectives. You know why? Because each one is important.

Richard Branson, chairman of Virgin Galactic, is a prolific generator of quotes. One that I like, especially because it recognizes the real folks, those on the front lines, is:

An exceptional company is one that gets all the little details right. And the people out on the front line, they know when things are not going right, and they know when things need to be improved. If you listen to them, you can soon improve all those niggly things which turn an average company into an exceptional company.

Now the questions become more numerous for all committee structures, such as:

- What is the purpose for each committee?
- How many committees should there be?
- What should be the membership size of each committee?
- Who would be best to serve on them?
- How often should they meet?

And probably a half dozen other foundational questions.

By the way, I suggest that you create a comprehensive list of questions for each committee agenda. Answering them will make the path much clearer to committee members, a result that will save great time and effort. If you do so up front, you will avoid unexpected gaps appearing.

If you are just putting your organization together, then you are pretty much beginning with a clean slate. If you have been in operation for a while, then you probably already have committees or equivalents (task forces, panels, bureaus, commissions, councils or other).

I am against riding a wobbly bike. If you are either forming your organization or not certain that it is optimally structured, I strongly suggest that you have a planning session that starts from zero. Forget what exists, if anything, and ask yourself this question: 'What functions need to be addressed in order for our organization to succeed?' There are many, many tools that you can use to answer this question, including traditional brainstorming, mindmapping, affinity charting and others. [My website will suggest a few others.] As an aside, in the previous chapter, I gave you a starter list. Don't rely on it. Start from scratch and come up with your own.

Once you have done so, then see which ones coalesce. You should be able to take the list and boil it down to no more than six groups, hopefully fewer. That completed, you likely have identified your board and subordinate committees. Now it's a matter of defining clear objectives and approaches for each.

If you would like to run your draft past me, I would feel privileged to provide you with feedback on it.

KEY POINTS

1. Board and committee memberships require you to identify the fine line between using and abusing these individuals. Either extreme, underusing or overusing, is a mistake.

2. Whatever board committees you form, make certain that all participate on the endowments committee. That is your organization's future.

3. Committees like our Chairman's Advisory Panel (CAP) is a wonderful way to accomplish much and is a fertile ground for future board members.

4. Don't be afraid to create a new committee if the need is there. Although you don't want a reckless organizational chart, you do want to get the best out of yourself, your staff and your volunteers.

5. Make certain to value all members of your board. Remember that they are working with you because of their generous hearts.

"No one has ever become poor by giving."
Anne Frank

"It's not how much we give but how much love we put into giving."
Mother Theresa

"As you grow older, you will discover that you have two hands: one for helping yourself, the other for helping others."
Sam Levenson

"You have not lived today until you have done something for someone who can never repay you."
John Bunyan

"It is the apathetic person that sees the cause while the charitable person sees the need."
Shannon L. Alder

"Do good by stealth, and blush to find it fame."
Alexander Pope

"Mirrors were made for people who help others."
Gloria L. Kelley

VII

FINANCE AND FUNDRAISING

CASA/Kane County has five pillars: Advocacy, People, Process, Technology and Finance. I mention this because, as you can see, one of the five is Finance. The absence of one of these five, especially finance, will seriously curtail and eventually derail our journey. So let me address this for a bit.

One of my favorite sayings is "No money, no mission." It's cute and catchy but it is also immensely true. In the more vernacular, "If you ain't got it, you can't give it." For me, finance and fundraising go hand in hand. Not only do I believe that fundraising and finance go together but I also (strongly) contend that they are the top priority of any successful organization.

I have seen many non-profit organizations where finance and fundraising are disconnected. The results have been well short of stellar. But, with the right team in place, I have seen several of them bring finance and fundraising into alignment, enabling the organization to move forward smartly thereafter. If you don't have that written out in a plan of action (POA) of who does what by when, you are asking for major troubles. And, no less important, keep updating it. At all times, though, keep your heart and your mind on the mission. I'll have more to offer on POAs in the next two chapters.

Major Events

If we (or any organization) were to brainstorm fundraising events, we could likely come up with literally dozens. But spreading oneself too thin is foolish. We have five major fundraising events. In calendar order, they are:

1. Gala – March
2. Benefit Concert - May
3. Golf Outing - August
4. Clays Shooting Tournament - September
5. Superheroes Luncheon – November

[If you are interested in knowing more about any of these, please contact me at *info@glorialkelley.com* and I will gladly provide whatever information would be of value to you.]

I ask board members to become actively involved in whichever two of the five major fundraising events are most meaningful to them. Extenuating circumstances aside, it is my belief that if a board member cannot choose two with which to become invested, I have to seriously wonder if they are the right person to be on our board.

Fundraising 101

Fundraising uses the Pareto Principle, often known as the 80/20 Rule, Law of the Vital Few or Principle of Factor Sparsity. It states that, for many events, roughly 80% of the effects come from 20% of the causes. In other words,

20% of your donor population will provide 80% of your contributions. Clearly, with limited resources at your disposal, you need to focus on the essential 20%...not to the exclusion of the others but with added focus.

I call it "repeatable and replaceable." Your donor base is constantly changing. People leave, pass away, experience changes to their disposable income and find other interests. [Perhaps a loved one contracted a particular disease and now the donor wants to throw all his/her time, money and efforts into finding a cure for it.] It becomes essential that we constantly evaluate our donor base. We need to be well aware of the pulse of our donors. At the same time, we need to cultivate new relationships. Finding new donors means working with your engaged volunteers, staff and others to identify and cultivate contacts. Connecting with business owners, in particular, potentially means getting their employees involved. The three top charities in giving are alma mater, religious and charity (such as ours) dealing with child abuse, cancer or pets.

Some Rules of Thumb

1. Each event should have its own goals and budgets. This allows the team with primary accountability to operate more effectively and efficiently.

2. Don't let volunteers slide into the background. It's easy to do because there are a lot of worthy causes out there. Make certain that your volunteers feel significant and appreciated. When you think about it, if you had to pay for their time, it would likely amount to a lot of money. In our case, volunteers invest over 20,000 hours each year.

Just a gross calculation would estimate their time to be well over a quarter of a million dollars, not including other expenses, if they were our employees. We host several appreciation events for our volunteers as well as multiple smaller venues, coffees and lunches. This helps let them know how much they are valued and heard.

3. This next one is very important: Do not have a volunteer handle your financials. You are running a business. You will be audited to make certain that policies and procedures are in compliance with GAAP and other legal guidelines. Remember this: The buck stops with you. Get a dedicated professional to do your bookkeeping.

4. Have a logical and explainable flow of what happens. For example, our office administrator receives a donation and then enters it into the system to be accounted for with the proper acknowledgement letter to follow. Then we reconcile the donation to whatever solicited or unsolicited campaign from which it came. As you would suspect, everything donated works carefully through our financial recordkeeping system. But it is also recorded in our donor database. In this manner, we know more about each particular donor. Weekly reports are used to review accuracy, determine first time and repeat donors and assist us in calling to thank them.

As an aside, we make it a practice to ask first time donors how they heard about us. It shouldn't surprise you that

80-90% are relationship based. People give to people first, causes second. If we are able to share our story so that others can embrace our mission, then everyone wins.

5. Do not allow any fundraising event to take on a life of its own. Always, always, always remember that the purpose of the event is to raise money for the cause that your non-profit addresses. Everyone in your organization should keep your overarching objective well in mind. It is too easy to become enamored with one event. When that happens, it can become like putting all your eggs in one basket. Bad idea. I meet with our Advancement Team to discuss weekly and monthly reports. We make it a point to differentiate between campaigns, thus allowing us to see what is and isn't working. These discussions are essential in order to bring elements into alignment in building the needed momentum to reach our fundraising goals.

Sustainability

Sustainable is an interesting word. Of its many definitions, one strikes me: "To keep in existence; to prolong." Even though it sounds noble, in most cases, I push back at that. I prefer to overlay this thought: If you are not moving forward, the rest of the world is.

Robert Browning wrote: "Ah, but a man's reach should exceed his grasp/Or what's a heaven for?" In other words, we should always be striving for more on behalf of our non-profit's objectives. Sustainability is adequate, but certainly not exceptional.

Nevertheless, I continue to use the word sustainability because, in most circles, it does not represent underachieving an objective. There's no need to upset the apple cart if it isn't something important.

We have four dimensions when it comes to sustainability.

Strategic Planning Dimension: This defines our strategic objectives and performance measures. These provide evidence of whether or not our strategy is yielding increased profitability and decreased costs.

- Ensuring our vision and strategic goals for the organization

- Ensuring realistic strategies to achieve the vision and goals

- Modifying the vision, goals and strategies to remain realistic when implementing plans

Program Dimension: These are our internal processes. They represent the impact of the quality of service. They also help identify which internal processes operate with excellence in order to serve 100% of all abused and neglected children.

- Verifying what our volunteers truly need, versus what they only want

- Evaluating effectiveness and outcomes of programs to verify they are meeting needs

- Changing program methods, if needed, to improve quality in order to meet the needs of the children we serve

Personnel Dimension: Here we have our internal operations that are based on financial cause and effect relationships. They address how CASA Kane County must appear to our donors and volunteers in order to fulfill the organization's mission.

- Ensuring staff has sufficient expertise, training and resources to provide for programs
- Ensuring staff members are maximizing their resources to provide programs
- Ensuring redundancy and succession planning for staff in case people leave

Financial Dimension: This is the learning and growth that enables the other three perspectives to achieve their objectives. It defines what type of staff and system we have in order to achieve the mission, support the internal processes and make certain that we are serving 100% of all children.

- Identifying how much funding (fees and/or fundraising) is needed to offset expenses
- Doing adequate prospect research to identify all likely sources of funds
- Allocating sufficient funding to administration and programs
- Tracking expenditures and revenues to promptly address financial priorities and issues
- Following policies to establish adequate reserves and to do contingency planning

Final Thoughts

As the leader (or one of the leaders) of your organization, you simply cannot be good at everything and you cannot become deeply involved in everything. But most of us want to do both. It took me a long time to realize two things. First, I am not an SME (subject matter expert) in everything. In fact, my expertise is rather limited. Second, I cannot be actively involved in every step of every campaign. There simply aren't enough hours in the day and, much as I sometimes wish I could, I don't have the energy to run 24/7.

Instead, you need to pick and choose. You need to surround yourself with the right people, help set the direction, recognize what they are doing, check what they are doing and trust in them. At times, you will be able to pick up an oar and help row the boat. But it wouldn't have worked well if the Viking leader was stuck in the galley.

Take a look in the appendix for "Changing the Culture from Fundraising to Philanthropy." I think that you will find it interesting and valuable.

KEY POINTS

1. In order to maximize your finance and fundraising, write (and update) a Plan of Action. Be specific in incorporating *who* will do *what* by *when*.

2. Identify your major fundraising events. Don't have so many that you can't provide the right level of focus on each one. Remember that you don't want fatigue from your loyal donor base.

3. Make certain that your board members are actively involved with one or two of your fundraising events.

4. Don't overlook your current donors while looking for new ones. Balance "repeatable and replaceable."

5. Don't take your volunteers for granted. They are the ones who make every event successful. Be certain to carve out activities that recognize the phenomenal work that they are doing.

6. Your financials need to be handled by full-time professionals. Nothing should get in the way of accurate reporting, for your purposes and for government reporting purposes.

7. When it comes to sustainability, establish your 'house' on firm pillars. [We have five, detailed earlier.] Assess your progress with each one.

"A goal without a plan is just a wish."
Antoine de Saint-Exupéry

*"The time to repair the roof is
when the sun is shining."*
John F. Kennedy

"Progress should be the product of the process."
Yohann Dafeu

*"If you don't know where you are going,
you'll end up someplace else."*
Yogi Berra

*"If you quit on the process,
you are quitting on the result."*
Idowu Koyenikan

*"Our progress, the realization of our dreams,
and the quality of our life depend directly
on the level of our commitment to the process."*
Dr. Prem Jagyasi

*"Knowing our destination is essential.
But we must also keep our eyes on the path."*
Gloria L. Kelley

VIII

PLANNING AND PROCESSES

I've touched on planning and processes in several places earlier in this book. However, there are a few things that I would like to confirm as well as some things that I would like to introduce. Simply stated, planning and processes are the skeleton of your non-profit body. As humans, we wouldn't be much without our skeleton. As organizations, we wouldn't be much without these two functions either. Very importantly, they need to work hand in hand.

I have a saying on my office wall that reads: "Failing to Plan is Planning to Fail." It was written by Benjamin Franklin and I used it in the introduction to Chapter 2. It is the first thing I read when I walk into my office. Although I have been told that I can be a little obsessive about this, I think about the planning process with my team at all times.

Using Time Wisely

In 1916, Henri Fayol defined the five functions of management: planning, organizing, commanding, coordinating and controlling. Nowadays, as you well know, the sophistication and terminology have changed fairly dramatically…much for the good but also a bit too much for the ego of authors.

Any undertaking has two components: (**1**) *Where* you are going; and (**2**) *How* you get there. One of those two without the other promises failure. Planning deals mostly with where you are going. Processes deal mostly with how you get there, what is now popularly referred to as execution.

Stephen Covey, in his book The Seven Habits of Highly Effective People, addresses time management. He illustrates his points with a four cell time management matrix. He immediately dismisses two of the cells that deal with *unimportant* matters. But he surprises the reader by advocating that they focus on the important/not urgent cell rather than the important/urgent cell. It's not intuitive. If there is a fire, we need to put it out, not sit on the porch and think of things that might happen tomorrow, the next day or the next week. Right?

Wrong. Leaders need to be focused on the tomorrows. If they do so, the urgent items become less numerous while the important items get more time and attention. Urgent items cannot be ignored but, by the same token, they cannot gobble up valuable resources in the moment. One of your most critical tasks will be to spend maximal time in the important/not urgent cell while minimizing the important/urgent cell. Where possible, your team needs to put out the fires, calling you in only when they run into insurmountable obstacles.

Who, What and When

In our organization we create a list for every project, big or small: *Who does what by when?* We don't conclude meetings until we have clearly and unequivocally completed this list. I call it a Plan of Action (POA). Then, after the meeting, one person is assigned the task of confirming this list to all who were in attendance, adding those who will have responsibilities but were not able to participate.

The logic is simple: We prepare our people for success. Because there is never one person solely working on any important project at any given time, everything is a team collaboration. What we are seeking to do is to recognize all who participate without worrying about how the credit will be distributed.

Harry Truman had a plaque on his desk that read: "The Buck Stops Here." And he was right. On a smaller scale, as executive director, I have the same approach and my team knows it. But if it is done correctly, *everyone* should feel the same, at least for their own domains. Each member must play an intricate role in the development and ownership of the organization's goals. If they don't, then they feel and act like mules, accepting the load without passion or concern...and sometimes being stubbornly unwilling to move.

When it comes to POAs, distinct and understood processes (with milestones) need to be in place for success to happen. This is very similar to Bruce Tuckman's four stages of group development: forming – storming – norming – performing. He pointed out that these stages were all necessary in order for a team to grow, face up to challenges, tackle problems, find solutions, plan work and deliver results. Our process follows.

Five Steps

We follow a five-step process in the formation, execution and evaluation of any undertaking. It looks like this:

1. ***Developing a strategic vision*** of where the organization needs to head and what its future product/market/customer/technology focus should be. This area provides long-term direction and infuses the organization with a sense of purposeful action.

2. ***Setting objectives to spell out performance expectations.*** Having a balanced scorecard approach for measuring company performance entails setting both financial and strategic objectives.

3. ***Crafting a strategy to achieve the objectives*** and move the organization along the strategic course that has been charted. Typically, this is more of a top-down than bottom-up strategy, serving as a guide to develop lower level managers.

4. ***Implementing and executing the chosen strategy efficiently and effectively.*** This is where the rubber meets the road, so to speak. Saying that you are going to do XYZ and doing XYZ can be on different sides of the planet. You cannot let that happen.

5. ***Evaluating performance and initiating corrective adjustments.*** This phase is the trigger point for deciding if you should continue

or change anything about what you are doing or how you are doing it.

Your Environment

Some people foolishly propose that non-profits don't have competitors. Of course we do! Just the same as a consumer determines which product to buy in a grocery store, so sponsors and volunteers determine which non-profits to support. Quite frankly, if you don't know your environment, your competitors and your associated position in that environment, the likelihood of you achieving your organization's ambitions are next to nil.

For my organization, there are seven key questions that form the framework for thinking strategically about the ocean in which our ship sails. They are:

1. What are the community's dominant economic features?

2. What competitive forces exist and how strong is each force?

3. What forces drive non-profit changes?

4. What market positions do non-profit rivals occupy?

5. What strategic moves are rivals likely to make?

6. What are the key factors for future competitive success?

7. Does our outlook look favorable to attain greater organizational capacity?

Practical Application

Alan Lakein is known for his time management tools and quotes. One quote which I very much like is: "Planning is bringing the future into the present so that you can do something about it." Isn't that good? One of the devices that I did not introduce in the chapter on Leadership Tools is called Backwards Imaging. My covering it here may provide you with a very valuable way for you to bring "the future into the present."

Backwards imaging has you assembling the team that will be working on an undertaking (i.e., before it gets underway). You create a hypothetical scenario for them. "Let's say that, in three years (after the projected completion date for this undertaking), a journalist is here from a prestigious publication. He/she wants to interview you because this was the absolute greatest example of how any undertaking was ever completed. What reasons would you give him/her?"

After a bit of laughter and clowning around, your team would probably list several distinct factors. They will likely include things common to all successful teams, such as communication, collaboration, time management and resources. They will also likely include things that might be unique to this particular project, such as proprietary software, patents and previous experience on a project like this.

Now comes the value of this tool. Once you have completed the list, you ask one leading question: "What do we have to do to make certain that we succeed employing these features?" The discussion that follows, especially the inventory that you create from it, becomes both a roadmap as well as operational guidelines for your success.

Once again, it's called backwards imaging and should find a place in one of your leadership tool belt pouches.

Final Thoughts

Formulating direction and then carrying it out is as challenging a responsibility as one can experience in leading an organization to achieve greater success. The benefits and vulnerabilities are enormous. Going after either, much less both, in a happenstance manner promises to create serious problems. This is no time for seat of the pants leadership.

The more systematic you are in your approach, the more likely you will achieve your objectives. That's because you and your team will better understand your destination, get maximal meaningful input, be better prepared for obstacles and be working together much more cohesively. When that happens, of course, leadership is so fulfilling.

"Sometimes life brings you full circle to a place you have been before just to show you how much you have grown."
Unknown

"Individually, we are one drop. Together, we are an ocean."
John F. Kennedy

"It always seems impossible...until it's done."
Nelson Mandela

"Completion is a goal but we hope it is never the end."
Sarah Lewis

"The main cause of failure is the habit of stopping before completion."
Idowu Koyenikan

"Success is not final; failure is not fatal: It is the courage to continue that counts."
Winston Churchill

"For many things, success is defined by what you do for others."
Gloria L. Kelley

IX

BRINGING IT
FULL CIRCLE

You may remember my saying in an earlier chapter "No money, no mission." It's one of my favorites. But there is another that we should all remember, as well: "No change, no progress." That's part of the reason that I wrote this book. Hopefully, it gives you the opportunity to confirm things that you are doing, question things that you are doing, look at things that you're not doing and make changes as you see fit. If I achieved that, then I will consider my efforts successful. If I contributed to your reinvigoration, then I will consider my efforts very successful. And if I inspire you to participate in my Website, then I will consider it an over-the-top success.

What Should You Do?

Like me, you have things to share. Perhaps it's involvement in my Website – tools, quotes or other contributions. Or, maybe, it's an article for a magazine.

Perhaps it's an industry publication or even a publication in the field of leadership. Maybe it's a conference lecture. Maybe it's teaching a class. It might even be a book. The point is: Look for ways to both learn and share. If you do so, both you and others will benefit.

I can't tell you what kind of leadership style you should employ. [I hope that you spent productive time defining your style in Chapter 2.] Your personality and situation differ from that of others. In *Hamlet*, Polonius says to his 18 year old son, Laertes: "To thine own self be true." Although not quite so eloquently, that's what I am encouraging you to do.

Most importantly, encourage your team members. Yes, there's constructive feedback necessary in any leadership environment. However, how you deliver it will determine its value, its impact and its longevity. Two examples follow:

1. "Can't you get it right! You need to do A, B and C. Now don't mess up again."

2. "I know that you can master this, although it's not overly easy. Remember to do A, B and C. Now let me see you master it."

You don't have to be a rocket scientist to see that you catch more flies with honey than you do with vinegar.

Eating the Elephant

Every leader has to balance urgency with patience. In Stephen Covey's 7 Habits of Highly Effective People, he devotes one chapter to each of the seven. The third habit is "Put first things first." This is primarily a chapter on time management. You'll need to read it (and the entire book, I'd suggest) but here is one of his major points: If you spend all your time putting out fires, you'll feel busy but you'll not be leading. Instead, if you can, delegate firefighting to your team and focus on more important things that will benefit from adequate or even extra preparation. The only way that you can do this is by better use of your time.

Although it's admirable for you to want to knock out opportunities or problems right away, some cannot be devoured in one sitting. Consider this when scheduling what you and your team can and should do. Many things take time. If you lead wisely, you'll know which to attack aggressively and which will have better results from a more strategic approach.

The Elephant in the Room

Speaking of elephants, one of the best things that you can do as a leader is to surface issues that others are unwilling to address. This takes courage and appropriate timing. I see a lot of (supposed) leaders who simply wish uncomfortable things would go away. They will wait, wait, wait and then it is often too late.

If your team knows that no subject is off limits with you, you will avoid major problems, likely major catastrophes, as well. Here's an awful conversation that one might hear between two team members: "The boss' pet project is doomed to failure. But I'll tell you what: I'm not gonna be the bearer of bad tidings. He might shoot the messenger and I'm not getting paid enough for that."

On the other hand, here's a similar conversation: "It's the boss' pet project and it looks headed for failure. I have some suggestions and I know the boss will appreciate receiving them, whether or not she adopts them."

It's the same scenario except for the fact that, in the second version, there is a chance to salvage the situation.

Final Thoughts

I still have a million thoughts of things that I want to share with you. However, as with any project, there is a time to freeze development and go with what you have produced. That's where I am right now.

But that's why I developed *www.glorialkelley.com*, my Website. I hope that it will pick up where this book left off. Its best chance of doing that will be if you contribute to it. Please do.

Thank you so much for taking the time to read this. I welcome your feedback and ideas.

APPENDIX

TEN FOR GREATNESS
Board Member Characteristics

By Gloria Kelley
(with Tom Berliner)

Over the years, I have spoken with many executive directors of non-profit organizations. When asked what they feel is the heartbeat of their organization, I get a myriad of responses. This both does and does not amaze me. On the one hand, our NFP world is as disparate as can be. The engine for one may not be the engine for another. On the other hand, our NFP world shares the common purpose of making life better for others. In our case, it is advocating for the best interests of abused and neglected children within the juvenile court system. Other entities have similarly noble objectives.

But one common thread that I have found throughout successful organizations is well-used and valued boards, be they called directors, trustees or whatever. With the right board, there are few pinnacles that are unattainable.

How does one create a board such as the one that CASA Kane County now boasts? I can firmly state that it is planned, not happenstance. Jim Collins, in his book Good to Great, uses the metaphor of a bus – getting the right people on the bus, getting them into the right seats and removing those who need to find another bus.] But who are the right people?

Let me share with you what I have found to be the major characteristics that we look for in a board member. It has taken us a while to find the right formula and the right people, but we consider ourselves very fortunate to have the board that now governs our organization.

1. **Passion** – If a potential board member does not zealously believe in our mission, then it is not a good fit…no matter what other characteristics he or she possesses.

2. **Business Savvy** – Board membership should not be a nominal appointment, one that is solely for recognition purposes. Board members need to be able to help row the boat, so to speak.

3. **Caring** – It always amazes me when I meet someone on another organization's board who doesn't have the compassion gene, as I like to call it. Behavioral skills are essential.

4. **Unique Skills** – If everyone on your board is good at the same thing, you are in for a lot of trouble. You want breadth and depth.

5. **Experienced** – Although in rare cases someone who lacks significant experience may contribute something special to your board, you'd best think about the big picture and the long term before adding them.

6. **Well-networked** – Although the author is unknown, most of us are familiar with the following quote: It's not what you know but who you know that counts. A board that is well-connected can resolve a plethora of obstacles.

7. **Coordinated** – Boards are addressing important and difficult issues. It is critical that members be focused on the optimal solution to each issue, not on whether they have won or lost a debate with their colleagues.

8. **Expressive** – Board members are not there to rubberstamp decisions made by the management team. They need to proactively support or challenge what comes before them.

9. **Ego Second** – We expect our board members to check their credentials at the door. We want their input from the perspective of what is best for those we serve, not what enhances the member's status.

10. **Financial Support** – My mantra is: No money, no mission. I smile when I write this because I am frequently teased about it. But, in our world, that's pretty much true. We expect board members to make a financial commitment to our mission within their means to do so. There is wide disparity in what each member contributes but it demonstrates the right kind of dedication.

CHANGING THE CULTURE
From Fundrasing to Philanthropy

By Gloria Kelley

Charity is a limiting concept that tends to be crisis-oriented and indicative of a weakness of some sort. This ultimately leads to the "tin cup" syndrome of fundraising (i.e., begging, impulsive, emotional, and, worst of all, token in nature). Those were the old days!

Philanthropy, however, is a much broader concept, the goal of which is to systematically solve problems. It is based on carefully thought out plans, building on previous successes, focusing on the community and benefiting our children, organization and community. In a philanthropic culture, everyone in the organization is comfortable with the two definitions of ROI: the traditional "return on investment" and the mission focused "results, outcomes and impact."

Consider the following as we educate, transform and make the shift from fundraising to a philanthropic culture:

1. The board, leadership, other committees, staff and volunteers truly understand the meaning of *philanthropy*. A new concept? No, actually a very old one, and a critical funding motivator for almost all donors.

2. When someone calls to make a donation, the administrative assistant to the supervisor knows who you are and what to do. All staff needs to know how to recognize and handle potential donors. Think customer service, competition and internal cooperation.

3. Accountability is something that we live by, rather than just paying lip service to it. The number one reason donors stop giving is because they don't think their gift was used as intended or promised. Being accountable in all aspects to our donors is essential.

4. CASA's primary role is not fundraising; it is building the philanthropic culture so that philanthropic relationships can survive and thrive. Our role is not to *get donors* nor is it to *raise money*. It is to build relationships that result in the formation of philanthropists. Outcomes to meet the mission which is raising philanthropic dollars is what we all need to prioritize.

5. CASA's leadership understands and acknowledges the difference between philanthropy advancement and fundraising. Philanthropy is the motivating value; development is the management of a systematic and strategic program and fundraising is the action. They are distinct but connected.

6. CASA has strong and motivating philanthropic values and communication. We strive to engage everyone every day so that all of us are consistently asking ourselves: Are we doing enough and are we prioritizing relationships?

7. Advancement is a core function that is long-term, strategic and responsive to community needs. Advancement is critical to fulfilling our organizational mission. It is a core part of your strategic thinking, planning, direction and action.

8. ***Fundraising is everyone's job.*** It simply doesn't work if fundraising is done in isolation. Everyone has a role, be it ambassador, enthusiastic communicator, connector, cultivator, solicitor, steward or some combination thereof.

9. One hundred percent of the board makes annual philanthropic gifts to our organization. Furthermore, the board demonstrates its ownership of fundraising, and all board members participate in fundraising, but not all in the same way. It is very hard to ask others to support the mission if the leaders of our organization are not making annual, meaningful gifts. I work to encourage board members to make it one of their top three philanthropic priorities and to be able to lead with both passion and demonstrated commitment.

10. Donors and volunteers in all areas are viewed as stakeholders in our organization. They should not be thought of as necessary, burdens, rich, your best friends, targets or nuisances. They are stakeholders who have invested because they care about what the organization does.

FOR YOUR NOTES: